T0368483

Balboa Press books may be ordered through booksellers or by contacting:

Balboa Press
A Division of Hay House
1663 Liberty Drive
Bloomington, IN 47403
www.balboapress.com
1 (877) 407-4847

ISBN: 978-1-5043-9731-5 (sc)
978-1-5043-9732-2 (e)

Library of Congress Control Number: 2018901544

Print information available on the last page.

Balboa Press rev. date: 03/01/2018

BALBOA.
PRESS
A DIVISION OF HAY HOUSE

A Ladybug Called Lily

Collection 1

By Barbara Rose Sumner

Illustrated by Cecil Gocotano

Table of Contents

Acknowledgments

To my three grandchildren, Tarin, Julian and Eden, who embraced me as their *visiting storyteller* over the many years during their young childhood, thank you for the inspiration to write **A Ladybug Called Lily**, my first children's book.

To my mother Rose, my daughter Treska and my brother Larry, thank you for your support and encouragement.

To Mark, my distinguished hero, thank you for sharing my vision and helping me to realize my dream.

Prologue

Lily is a very special ladybug. Her parents named her Calla Lily after the beautiful flowers that grew in the garden where she was hatched. Everyone prefers to just call her "Lily". Unlike the other newly hatched ladybugs, Lily is a bright pink color, but what makes her even more special is the halo, circle of light, that surrounds her entire body. As the black spots on her back become more visible, her pink color and her halo become even brighter. The ring of light is always with her. The elder ladybugs, also called ladybird beetles, thought that something was terribly wrong with Lily, but they soon realized that there was something amazing about her.

The many beautiful gardens where Lily frolics about with her friends is filled with a variety of brightly colored flowers, warm-green bushes, red, pink and golden shrubs neatly arranged around small rock beds and ponds. This blissful place is paradise for many birds and insects. In this picturesque setting, Lily experiences many memorable encounters and learns many important life lessons.

A Ladybug Called Lily

Collection 1

Story 1

The Rescue

The sun was beaming through the thatch-roof of the tiny hut where Lily lived with her mother and father. Lily opened one eye and gazed at the sunlight. She quickly rolled out of her bed of leaves and headed toward the kitchen. "Good morning, mom," she sang excitedly. Her halo lit up like a neon light.

"Good morning Lily. What are you so excited about this morning?" Before Lily could respond, her mom continued. "Um-m-m… Could it be this tasty breakfast that I've prepared for you, or is it all of the chores that you have to do?"

"Oh, mom. You're so funny," Lily chimed. They both laughed.

"I was hoping that I could have a picnic lunch with some of my friends later. Is that okay?" Lily had not thought about her chores.

"Well, you know the rules." She gave Lily her "no nonsense" look.

"I know. Work first and then play." Lily's halo became dim.

A few hours later, Lily had finished all of her chores, but as soon as she was done packing her picnic sack, she heard a loud clap of thunder. "Oh no! Mom, was that thunder?"

"Yes honey." Her mom sighed. "I'm sorry."

Lily mumbled to herself, "There goes my picnic." Her circle of light was barely visible as the rain came down in a rush.

Meanwhile, Lily's friends had just made it to the picnic area as the rain started to pour down. Cindy, Debbie, Anna, Peter and Tony were surprised by the rain. While rushing to find shelter, a large tree branch had fallen in front of them.

Someone screamed, "We're trapped!" Darkness was quickly moving in their direction.

"What are we going to do?" Cindy's voice quivered.

"We'll figure something out." Tony tried to sound brave, but he felt nervous.

"I'm scared." Anna whimpered softly.

"So am I." Debbie snuggled closer to Anna.

"Everyone stay calm!" Peter shouted. "Let's see if we can push the branch."

"It's too big for us to move it," admitted Peter after only one attempt.

Tony yelled, "Let's get under that big leaf at the end of the branch!"

A short time later, some of the elder ladybugs were out searching for them. They traveled several feet passing the garden of roses and golden barberry bushes. Suddenly the darkness covered them. Beyond the path, they could hear someone singing a sweet melody. "Do you hear that?" One of the elders asked. "It's coming from the green leafy bushes." They hurried over to the area as fast as their little legs could carry them.

Safe from the storm, under their tiny hut, Lily and and her family had just finished their dinner. As usual, Lily was the "after dinner" entertainment. She loved singing and her family looked forward to being her audience.

"Hello." The elder ladybugs spoke in unison. "Excuse us for interrupting your evening."

"It's quite alright!" Lily's mom responded. "Why are you out walking in the rain?"

"We're looking for some of the little ones that live by the pink geraniums. They may be lost, and they'll never find their way home in the dark," explained one of the elders.

"Mom and Dad, may I help to look for them?" The halo around Lily became brighter as she eagerly awaited their reply.

"That's a great idea, Lily!" Her parents nodded their heads as they answered together.

"We'll come along too," her father continued. "You can lead the way!"

Lily's halo cast a bright light along the path they traveled. "Let's check by the daylilies. That's where we had planned to meet," announced Lily. The heavy rain had become a soft sprinkle. A cool breeze blew past them as they danced around and over the glistening puddles of water.

Beyond the regal evergreen trees, the echo of tiny voices could be heard.

"Help! Help!"

"Wait. Stop! Did you hear that?" Lily's dad put up his right hand. "Someone's calling for help!"

"It's coming from behind that tree branch," shouted one of the elders.

"Follow me!" Lily raced across the tree branch as fast as she could.

Everyone quickly followed behind her. On the other side of the tree branch, they found the little ladybugs tightly clinging to one of the leaves on the branch.

"Look!" shouted Tony. "They found us!"

The little ladybugs screamed with joy, "Hooray! Hooray!"

All at once, the rain stopped and one bright star shone down on them. "Let's go home!" Lily sang. "Just follow my light and we'll get there safely." She started singing one of her favorite songs. As the group marched along singing, all the other insects and birds began adding their own unique harmony to Lily's beautiful voice. The magic of music was alive throughout every garden.

A Ladybug Called Lily

Collection 1

Story 2

Helping Friends

Beyond the garden of sweet smelling flowers, perched high in a flowering pear tree, two robins, Tom and Tina, were chatting about a special ladybug called Lily. They enjoyed telling anyone who was new to the garden about Lily. A beautiful butterfly with bright yellow wings landed on the branch next to them.

"Hi. My name is Belinda. Do you mind if I rest here?" She spoke so softly and carefree.

"Of course not," replied Tina. She was so happy to have a guest.

"Thank you. I overheard you talking about a special ladybug. Can you tell me about her?" Belinda's wings began to flutter revealing tiny brown specks.

"Oh. Let me start!" Tom interrupted Tina as she was about to speak. "Lily has a bright circle of light around her always.'" He paused for a moment. "It's been with her all of her life!" The pitch of

Tom's voice rose as he added this very important detail.

"She is so helpful to everyone!" Tina spoke up quickly before Tom could continue. "And she sings beautifully!"

"One day I would like to meet her. Thank you for letting me rest here. I'll be on my way now. Goodbye." Belinda abruptly flies away before either Tina or Tom could get out another word.

"Is it true that when a yellow butterfly flies around you, it brings you happiness and prosperity?" Tom wondered aloud. Tina lifted her wings up and shook her head to convey her cluelessness.

Over near the pink rose bushes, Lily was playing "hide and seek" with some of her friends.

"You're it!" Lily shouted after tagging Anna and racing between the short blades of grass.

"Oh, Lily, you're too fast for us," complained Henry. "We'll never catch you!"

Lily laughed teasingly as she continued to run as fast as she could. "Catch me if you can! Catch me if you can!"

"Don't tease us Lily!" Anna shouted while trying to catch her breath.

"Where is she?" Henry was feeling defeated.

"Let's look for her light," suggested Amy.

"That's a great idea!" Anna happily replied. "We should have no trouble at all finding her, but we have to keep quiet so she doesn't know we're getting close."

The three friends hurried across the small grassy hills. In the distance, they could see a bright light. "I think I see her hiding behind that barberry bush over there." Henry whispered as he pointed in the direction of the bush.

"Oh, I can see her too." Anna softly chimed in and dashed off toward the light, but before she had moved an inch, the light had disappeared. "Oh, no! I don't see the light anymore," whined Anna.

They looked at each other, sighed and scurried off in the direction of the rows of leafy green and white hostas. "Maybe she's under there!" Amy pointed to one of the leaves.

"I see something moving." Henry tried to minimize his excitement by keeping his voice as low as he could. Amy and Anna followed closely behind him, but they soon realized that what Henry saw moving was not Lily at all. Instead, it was a giant wasp, a main predator of the ladybug. They were overwhelmed with fear and could not move or speak.

Suddenly, a light appeared behind the wasp. It was Lily. Her halo began blinking as she cautiously crawled closer to the wasp and bit one of its back legs. The wasp flinched and turned around. Its eyes caught a glimpse of Lily hurrying away as fast as her tiny legs could take her. The wasp took flight chasing Lily in and out and around the rows of hosta plants. Whenever it would get closer to the light that circled her, she would take off with even greater speed moving in a different direction.

"Wow! Look at Lily go!" Amy exclaimed.

"Yeah. She is really fast," added Henry.

They were feeling somewhat relieved as Lily lead the wasp farther and farther away from them until they spotted a family of bees circling around a bed of daisies. "Oh, no!" Anna cried. "Lily is heading straight in the path of the bees!"

The three ladybugs nestled closely together and anxiously watched Lily dashing past the swarm of bees and the wasp following close behind her.

Unexpectedly, something astonishing happened. The bees flew after the wasp and began to circle it. The wasp recognized what was happening. Like a jet, it made a sudden change in its flight plan and hastily flew off in a different direction.

After a few minutes, Lily had made it to the rose of Sharon bush. She was gasping for air.

"Are you okay?" A soft voice was heard coming from the bush.

Lily looked up and saw the most beautiful butterfly that she had ever seen resting on one of the violet roses of the tree. Her yellow color was dazzling.

"I'm being chased by a wasp!" Lily replied and took a deep breath.

"You don't have to worry. The wasp is no longer chasing you. I saw a swarm of bees chasing it off in the other direction." The butterfly reassured her. "My name is Belinda, and you must be Lily."

"How do you know my name?" Lily was feeling quite puzzled.

"Two of the robins told me all about you." Belinda flew down from the tree and flew around Lily. "I'm so happy that I had a chance to meet you!"

The sound of Belinda's voice made Lily feel very relaxed. She closed her eyes for only a moment. When she opened them, she watched Belinda flying away. Her wings seem to sparkle beneath the bright rays of sunlight. Lily smiled to see such a beautiful sight, and when she heard the echoes of her friends' cheers in the background, her halo was all aglow.

A Ladybug Called Lily

Collection 1

Story 3

The Surprise Guest

Lily tried hard to dismiss the blue jays' chirping in the tree above her. "What could they be chattering about?" She thought out loud. "I thought this would be a perfect spot for me to sunbathe." The chirping faded as the birds flew away. She snuggled in closely to the center of the sunflower. This was her special time alone, and she didn't want anything or anyone to interrupt her. She found the warmth of the sun both relaxing and energizing. Unfortunately, after only a few minutes of relaxation, Lily was abruptly disturbed when she heard Anna approaching and calling her name.

"Lily! Lily! Where are you?"

"Oh-h-h." Lily sighed and waited a few minutes before replying.

"Lily! Lily! Lil-l-l-y!" Anna began to sing.

"I'm over here in the bed of sunflowers!" Lily shouted.

"Keep talking Lily! I can follow the sound of your voice!" Anna shouted back.

Lily was very annoyed, but she tried not to show it. "Okay, Anna. I'm just past the purple tulips and across from the red rocks!"

"I see you now!" Anna raced over to the sunflower to join her friend. "I have some exciting news! I bet you can't guess what it is."

24

"Anna, come on. You know I don't like playing the guessing game." Lily had revealed her annoyance. "Just tell me what's so exciting."

"There's a new ladybug in the garden! Her name is Jenny. She and her family live near the pink geranium patch. She has a brother named Tommy. He's really cute!" Anna took a deep breath and only paused long enough to allow Lily to respond. "Well… Isn't that exciting?" Anna's excitement was fading.

Lily's response showed little interest or emotion. "Well, if you think it's exciting, it's exciting."

"Don't you want to come and meet her?" Anna scratched her head. She always did this when she was confused.

"Not now Anna. I'm enjoying my quiet time lying here in the sun," whispered Lily softly as she rolled onto her back and closed her eyes.

Anna was speechless. She was bothered by Lily's behavior, but she refused to give up. "I told her all about you and your special "halo"! She is very eager to meet you!"

"That's nice." Lily sighed deeply. "I am sure that I will meet her soon enough."

"Okay, Lily. I guess I'll see you later." Anna felt very disappointed and slowly crawled away.

The next day, Lily felt awful about how she had treated Anna. Her mom always told her, "Treat others the way you would want them to treat you". Anna was one of Lily's best friends and she valued her friendship.

She decided to go over to the pink geranium garden to look for Anna and the new neighbor, Jenny. After crawling for several inches and not seeing anyone, she came across a couple of humming birds playing in a pond. "Excuse me!" Lily waved at them trying to get their attention. "Hello! Have you seen any of the little ladybugs?" They didn't answer. "Where is everyone?" She was feeling frustrated. After circling the geranium garden three times, she headed back home. Her halo became dim as it often did when she felt sad.

As Lily approached the rose garden, she saw Tony and Henry running across a small pond several feet ahead of her. She called out to them, "Tony! Henry!" They did not look back and soon disappeared from view. "No! No!" Lily cried. "Where did they go?" She raced along as fast as she could, following the path beyond the sunflowers. Instantly her halo became brighter when she heard the laughter of little ladybugs nearby. The giggles and squeals were blaring. "I must be getting closer." Lily felt reassured and filled with joy. She spotted all of her friends playing under the big oak tree. They were having a big feast.

Anna saw her first. "Hey, Lily! Come on over!"

"We're so glad that you could join us!" Amy ran over to greet Lily with a hug.

"What's going on?" Lily inquired curiously.

"We're having a welcome party for Jenny and her family," explained Anna.

"I thought you were tired of us and didn't want to be bothered."

"Why would you ever think that? You're my best friends!" Lily added thoughtfully.

Anna smiled and happily announced, "Our surprise guest has arrived!" As Jenny and all of the other ladybugs surrounded Lily, her halo gave off a bright yellow hue.

A Ladybug Called Lily

Collection 1

Story 4

We Are All Special

Lily was known as a very special ladybug among all of the creatures in and around the garden where she lived. It was not only because of the circle of light that surrounded her entire body, but also because of her beautiful singing voice. Whenever Lily was singing, the birds and other insects would pause to listen. The melody of her songs was uplifting and seem to bring joy to all. None of the other ladybugs displayed any vocal talents, and most of them appeared to lack the courage to even attempt to sing, except for one.

One sunny morning, this special ladybug made her unintentional singing debut. Three young robins were perched in a magnolia tree when they heard someone singing. "What is that awful noise?" the first robin inquired.

"It's coming from that patch of pink geraniums," replied the second robin.

"Let's get closer," the third robin insisted.

They flew closer and landed on a tree branch above the pink geraniums. It was Jenny, the ladybug whose family had recently moved into the garden. "Hey! What are you doing down there?" The first robin flew over and around Jenny. She was frightened and thought she would be gobbled up, but she soon realized that she was in no danger.

Jenny looked at them intently and proudly proclaimed, "I am singing one of my favorite songs!"

Then the second robin joined the first robin and together, they flew over and around her. "What? You call that singing?"

"You don't like my singing?" Her response was meek and barely a whisper.

All three robins were now flying over and around her. "No!!!" They yelled altogether and promptly flew away.

At that moment, Lily was strolling nearby and spotted the robins overhead. Their wild laughter echoed throughout the garden. "I wonder what's going on?" The sound of laughter was soon overshadowed by the sound of someone sobbing. "Who's there?" Lily called out. No one responded. She scurried along in the direction of the pink geranium patch. The sobbing had become louder when she saw Jenny.

"Jenny! It's me, Lily." Jenny wiped away her tears as Lily approached her.

"What's wrong Jenny? Why are you crying?"

"I'm just feeling sad. That's all."

"Why?" Lily calmly inquired.

"Well…" Jenny hesitated. "I was minding my own business, singing one of my favorite songs, when these three robins started teasing me about how awful I sounded."

"What! That's really mean! I know your feelings are hurt Jenny," Lily tried to console her, "but you shouldn't let anyone upset you about your singing."

Jenny seem to perk up. "I guess I'm a little too sensitive," she stated softly.

"Everyone knows how much I love to sing," Lily politely interjected. "Singing makes me feel happy!" A big smile adorned Lily's face as her halo glowed a bright white.

"Really?" Jenny gleefully responded.

"Sure!" Lily was as excited as Jenny. "What's your favorite song? Let me hear you sing it."

"Do you want me to sing for you right now?" Before Jenny had hardly taken her next breath, she began to sing out the lyrics with an alarming intensity. She sang as loud as she could. Her vocal range was up and down, too high and then too low. With each screeching note, Lily's halo became dimmer. She resisted the urge to interrupt Jenny after deciding that would be impolite. What Lily thought would be a beautiful melody was instead a tune that was terribly off-key. Jenny's final note was almost too much to bear. It seemed to go on forever.

"How was that?" Jenny took a deep breath as she eagerly waited for Lily to comment.

"Well Jenny…" Lily paused briefly. "I like the song, but…"

"You didn't like my singing?" Jenny interrupted.

"Well, as I was about to say…" Lily paused briefly again. "I would like to help you improve your singing, if that's okay." Lily chose her words carefully to avoid hurting Jenny's feelings.

"Oh yes, Lily! I would love for you to help me! When can we start?" Lily was surprised by Jenny's eager response.

"If you have time, we can start now. Can you come over to my garden? It's my dinner time, but I'd love it if you can come for dinner." Then Lily added, "I hope you like sunbaked aphids."

"Yes, I do! They're my favorite! I need to check in with my mom first and then I will be right over." Jenny began singing her favorite song again as she happily skipped away. Lily took a deep breath, smiled, and blinked her beautiful eyelashes. A bright glow was all around her.

A Ladybug Called Lily
Collection 1

Story 5

Where's Lily?

After several gloomy, rainy days, it was finally a perfect weather day in the garden. The sweet songs of the robins and blue jays softly entertained everyone. Lily was up very early this sunny morning. She was eager to find a perfect spot to sunbathe. Usually she liked to sunbathe alone, but today she thought it would be nice if her mother could join her. "Mom!" Lily was quickly finishing up her breakfast.

"Ye-e-es, my darling Lily," her mom sang.

Lily smiled and her light glimmered. "Do you want to come sunbathing with me?" Lily crossed her two front legs and hoped her mom would say, "yes".

"Not today, sweetie. I have some errands to run."

"Ah-h-h. Okay." Her light flickered.

"I promise that I will go with you next time. Enjoy yourself. Okay? I love you."

"I love you too mom." Lily's halo became bright again.

A few minutes later, Lily was hurrying through the different gardens looking for her perfect spot. She soon eyed a large Shasta daisy with vibrant white petals. "Oh! Wow! A beautiful Shasta daisy." Lily knew, like everyone in the ladybug community, that Shasta daisies were special because they symbolize innocence, purity and cheerfulness. She scampered up the huge green stalk of the flower and made her way to the petals that were directly beneath the sunlight. Her halo began to glow brighter as the warmth of the sun blanketed her entire body. Suddenly a dark shadow blocked the rays of sun, and instantly Lily felt her body being carried upward. She helplessly clung to one of the petals. Within seconds, darkness completely surrounded her. "What's going on?" Lily murmured to herself. She was too afraid to yell. "I must stay calm. I must stay calm." She repeated these words over and over, but when her light became very dim, she became very worried. She realized that something or someone was moving the flower. The only thing she could do was to hold on to the petal even tighter.

Later that day, Jenny was on her way to the garden where Lily lived. She was very excited about how well her singing lessons with Lily were going. Although Lily was not expecting her, Jenny was hoping that Lily would be free to give her a lesson. She saw Lily's mom crawling nearby so she extended her short steps and ran in her direction. "Hel-lo Li-ly's- mom. How- are -you –to-day?" Jenny paused several times between the heavy breaths she took.

"Hi Jenny. I am doing well. How are you?"

"I am fine! Where's Lily?" Jenny asked anxiously.

"Well…" Lily's mom began. "She left some time ago to sunbathe. I thought she would be back by now."

"Oh. I'll check some of her favorite sunbathing spots." Jenny dashed off in the opposite direction humming a happy tune.

"When you find her, please tell her she needs to come home!" Lily's mom shouted in Jenny's direction, but wondered if she heard her.

Jenny hurried through many gardens and passed several beautiful flower beds. She stopped suddenly when she heard laughter and chatter in the distance. She followed the sound of the small voices to the foot of the magnolia tree.

"Tag! You're it!" The giggles grew louder.

Jenny saw Amy, Anna, Debbie, Tony and Henry running around the tree.

"Hello!" Jenny yelled, but they continued playing. "Hello everyone!" Jenny yelled louder this time. Henry and Amy stopped running and looked over toward Jenny.

"Hi Jenny!" They both shouted merrily. "Come play with us!"

"I can't play now. Have you seen Lily?"

"No!" Their responses were muffled with laughter.

"We've been here playing all morning," added Tony.

"Well, I have to find her. Her mom said that she left home earlier this morning to go sunbathing," explained Jenny.

Then Debbie suggested, "Let's help Jenny find Lily."

"Yeah. We'll help find Lily," agreed Tony.

"Hey. Listen everybody!" Their eyes were all on Amy. "I've got an idea! Let's check the flower gardens by the pond."

They all scampered off in the direction of the pond chanting, "Find Lily! Find Lily!"

A few feet away, Lily was still blanketed in darkness. As long as she felt fear, her halo remained dim. "Where am I?" Her eyes became teary. "How do I find the light?" The petal that she clung to began to shake. "What's going on?" Lily tried her best to stay calm and fight off the uneasiness that she was feeling. Suddenly she felt herself moving upward again. Then something wonderful happened. Lily could see the sunlight again. She patiently suffered through a few more quick, jerking movements when all at once everything became still. "I have to get home."

Without delay, she crawled down the stalk of the flower as fast as she could. At first, she was startled when she realized that her surroundings were different. "How did I get here?" Feeling bewildered, she hastily moved across the red rocks. "Oh-h-h-h!" She cried out, "I hope I can find my way home!"

For several minutes, she frantically traveled through many flower gardens when her pace abruptly slowed. "I think I hear something." She felt her heart skip a cautious beat and her circle of light blinked on and off.

"Find Lily! Find Lily!"

"Are those my friends?" Lily's light began to beam brightly. With tears running down her face, she rushed toward the sound of the voices.

"There's Lily!" Anna shouted pointing in the direction of the yellow dwarf daylilies.

"Lily! Lily!" The whole group screamed. They all surrounded her and started cheering, "Ya-ay! Ya-ay!" Lily was overcome with joy.

"Don't cry Lily." Jenny rubbed one of her tiny feet across Lily's head trying to console her. The cheering stopped. They huddled together for a big group hug.

"Where were you, Lily?" Henry asked anxiously.

Lily shook her head. "I'm not really sure." She was silent for a moment. "But it all started when…" They moved in closer to Lily to hear her story. A yellow glow covered her and spread out toward her friends. The birds in the garden hovered over the little ladybugs intently listening to Lily's story.

About The Author

Barbara Rose Sumner, a lifelong storyteller, embraced her love of writing over fifty years ago. Her first piece of writing, a poem entitled, "I Strive for Fame", was published in her elementary school newspaper.

This writer brings a wealth of ideas to her writing that she acquired from her childhood experiences growing up in Chicago, as well as her interactions with children during her thirty-seven years of teaching and her treasured experiences as the *visiting storyteller* to her three loving grandchildren. All of these experiences have been immeasurably valuable in helping this writer find her unique voice as an empathetic storyteller who can effectively relate to the varied social and emotional domains of her characters.

Printed in the United States
By Bookmasters